My Mommy is an Airman

Written and illustrated
by
Kirk and Sharron Hilbrecht

This book belongs to:

_____

10 9 8 7 6 5 4 3 2 1

ISBN 1-889658-36-7

This edition is produced in connection with Your Guardians of Freedom. This edition is not for resale.

My mommy is an airman.

Sometimes she gets up really early to exercise. Mommy says she has to exercise to stay in shape, and I help.

We do push-ups...

...and sit-ups.

Sometimes I ride my bike while mommy runs.

She irons her uniform every day so it will be nice and neat. It is green and has lots of pockets.

She polishes her boots, too. They are shiny and black, and a little too big for me...for now.

Mommy goes to work at an Air Force base. She works and trains to help people.

Mommy says she has to be ready for whatever job she might have to do. "The Air Force is busy these days."

"They feed hungry people...

...they keep an eye on things from space...

...they rescue people when they need help....

...and they take care of bad guys."

Sometimes mommy goes away for a long time. She packs up her uniforms, her gear, and her canteen, and she carries all of her things in a duffel bag.

Mommy says when she goes on a mission, it helps her learn to be a better airman, but I miss her when she's gone. I wish she had room enough for me.

Once, mommy went away for a very long time. My daddy helped me write letters to her, and I drew pictures so she could hang them up and think of us.

We baked cookies to send in mommy's care packages. Chocolate chip are her favorite. Mine too.

While she was gone, mommy wrote to me. I checked the mailbox every day.

When a letter came, my older sister read it out loud. Mommy always said she missed us.

When mommy finally came home, she gave us lots of hugs and kisses.

She was really dirty, but Daddy didn't make *her* take a bath.

Mommy's squadron likes to have picnics for the families to all get together and eat good food.

Mommy says, "It's important to get to know the other Air Force families. Mommies can be airmen and daddies can be airmen, but the *whole family* plays an important part in the Air Force family."

"These folks help support each other every day...especially when the unit is away."

I know lots of other kids from mommy's unit. We're friends and we like to play and do things together.

Sometimes we talk about what our moms and dads do that makes us proud.

Tyler's dad is an airlift pilot, and he flies really big planes all around the world.

Christina's mom is an Air Force doctor, and she fixes people...even kids from other Air Force families.

Michael's dad is an Air Force mechanic, and he fixes big trucks and keeps all the Air Force vehicles running great.

Ashley's dad is a Security Forces airman. He watches and protects the airplanes and people on base.

I'm proud that my mommy is an airman.

She helps make the world a safe place to live.